# FROM WHERE
# THE RIVERS COME

OTHER BOOKS AUTHORED, COAUTHORED, OR EDITED BY RICHARD SOLLY:

*The Way Home: A Collective Memoir*, Center City, MN: Hazelden, 1997.

*Call to Purpose: How Men Make Sense of Life-Changing Experience*, Center City, MN: Hazelden, 1995.

*Oh, Light Sleeper, Wild Dreamer*, anthology of students' poetry and prose, editor, St. Paul, MN: COMPAS, 1994–95.

*Journey Notes: Writing for Recovery and Spiritual Growth*, Center City, MN, and San Francisco, CA: Hazelden/Harper & Row, 1989.

# FROM WHERE
# THE RIVERS COME

POEMS

RICHARD SOLLY

HOLY COW! PRESS · DULUTH, MINNESOTA · 2006

## ACKNOWLEDGMENTS

I wish to express my gratitude for fellowships and grants from the Minnesota State
Arts Board, Bush Foundation, McKnight Foundation, Jerome Foundation, Loft
Literary Center, Iowa State University, Banff Centre for the Arts, and Blacklock
Sanctuary. I'm immensely indebted to Jay White for his untiring work on poems
in this collection, for his dogged encouragement, and our inspiring walks at our
usual place in the universe. Special thanks to my editor, Jim Perlman, Cheri Register,
Damian and Sandy McElrath, Pat Owen, David Cost, Jerry Flannery, Peter Canon,
my Wednesday night group, my family, and extraordinary daughter Rose. Finally,
my appreciation extends for the medical work of Bonnie Sue Rolstad, the heart-
work of Terry Robinson, and how eloquently they translate the strange mysteries of
both mind and body.

Many of these poems have previously appeared in the following publications:
*Green Mountains Review, The Healing Muse, Bellevue Literary Review, Minnesota
Medicine, Water-Stone, Mediphors, Poetry East, Common Journeys, Sutured Words,
Poet and Critic.*

Several poems in this collection have been translated into Japanese by Professor
Ryozo Morishita and Yumi Kawai and exhibited at the Nagoya City Archives.

Library of Congress Cataloging-in-Publication Data

Solly, Richard
From where the rivers come : poems / by Richard Solly
p. cm.
ISBN 0-9779458-1-2 (pbk. : alk. paper)
I. Title.
PS3619.O4328F76   2006
811'.6--dc22        2006048609

This project is supported, in part, by a grant from the Elmer L. &
Eleanor J. Anderson Foundation and by donations from generous individuals.

Holy Cow! Press titles are distributed to the trade by Consortium Book Sales,
1045 Westgate Drive, Saint Paul, Minnesota 55114.
Please visit our website: www.holycowpress.org.

Holy Cow! Press, PO Box 3170, Mount Royal Station, Duluth, Minnesota 55803

*for Rose*

*and*

*Jay White*

# Contents

I INTO THE WILD

| | |
|---|---|
| River of Coffee | 13 |
| Revisions | 15 |
| The Same Prayer | 16 |
| It's Not Music the Crow Plays | 18 |
| Mercy | 19 |
| White Point, Nova Scotia | 21 |
| A Violet | 22 |
| Please Note | 23 |
| Lilacs Scent Our Exile | 24 |
| Blue Strawberry | 26 |
| In Defense of Kneeling | 27 |
| Becoming a Carnivore | 29 |
| Love Letter to Lucifer | 32 |
| The Blossom and the Coffin | 33 |
| Into the Wild | 36 |
| Our Usual Place in the Universe | 38 |

II TWO BODIES

| | |
|---|---|
| A Crack in the Dark | 43 |
| The Plum | 44 |
| A Blood Race | 49 |
| Philoctetes | 50 |
| Right There | 51 |
| The Human Pincushion | 53 |
| Falling | 55 |
| Dynamite | 56 |
| Anatomical Wonders in Gibsonton, Florida | 57 |
| Mary | 58 |

Arse Poetic: A Defense                                          60

The Submarine                                                   62

The Anatomical Wonder Plays Dead in the Doctor's Office   63

White                                                           64

The Double                                                      66

Betting on Afternoon Light                                      67

Lazarus Comes Home                                              68

The Teacup                                                      70

The Immensity                                                   71

Two Bodies                                                      72


III  PRAYERS OF THE PEN                                         75


IV  TRUE NORTH

The Smell of Apples                                             83

A Horse Named Sex                                               84

The Bathtub                                                     85

Atlas Revisited                                                 86

End of Summer                                                   87

The Body Reproaches the Soul                                    88

What the Hats Whisper                                           90

Pilgarlic                                                       91

Laughing Falls                                                  93

Then Let Me Bring                                               96

Roses and Thorns, Pots and Pans                                 97

Shoelaces                                                       99

Why a Poem Ends in Death                                        100

True North                                                      101

Oil and Rags                                                    103

Notes                                                           107

About the Author                                                109

*All the rivers run into the sea; yet the sea is not full;*
*unto the place from whence the rivers come,*
*thither they return again.*

**ECCLESIASTES 1:7**

I

# INTO THE WILD

*Incline thy ear to me...*
*For my days pass away like smoke,*
*and my bones burn like a furnace.*

PSALM 102:2–3

# RIVER OF COFFEE

If only there were a river, as wide as the Mississippi
in St. Paul, black as this coffee, where a man might lug

his heart, lie down on the shore or wade to his hips,
and all the cracked cups, the pain he feels for his dead,

the woman he'll never touch again, the voices whispering
under his pillow, every mouth he kissed good-bye,

even the bobby pin found under his bed—all of it gathered,
so he might squeeze it like a sponge into the water,

squeeze his liver, his intestines, the memories lodged
like stones in the bile duct, squeeze every joy and sorrow

out of his cock, his body, into the wider body of the river
of coffee and irretrievable losses; a smoky, ink-black river

whose color absorbs all the dyes, bleaches, pigments
that memory and God spills into the heart, flowing

into eternity, because when we love, are loved,
we are paid in grief. The day empties, leaving only a breath,

while the river keeps deepening. We throw our chairs,
lamps, rings, scarves, photos, and stars into it, but they

keep washing ashore. Nothing is lost. A yellowed letter
found in a drawer unfolds moonlight in our room.

Forgetting will take us into eternity, where I picture myself
sitting with a cup, much like this one, steadying my hands,

the coffee containing the aroma of history, steaming,
never or slowly disappearing, sip by sip, my river.

# REVISIONS

It's the last hour. So much second guessing.
Which noun? Which verb? What word might persuade
at the door. Maybe another man with thicker hair, a body
he has no quarrel with, is better for you than the poem
I'm always erasing, rewriting, replacing this phrase
for that one, adjusting my collar. I buy lilies for you,
write a note, rewrite it three times. Everything's flawed.
Even the long-necked stems in white porcelain.
You've seen me sit at a table, nudge my chair closer,
lean back, negotiating time, distance. I prefer the sun
at another angle, the bedroom repainted, the garden weeded.
No. This is what I mean: we are poems, drafts, revised
by a kiss, hurt by nouns, defeated by a little birth
or death we never saw coming. We are a stream.
No single word ever the same, altered by currents, eddies,
a syntax of mud and straw. The water's end begins
the next poem, always unfinished, doubling back
to a lyrical pebble, splash of dissonance. Like sentences,
we once lay alongside each other and created the shore.
The wind rode across our bodies. Now, our hearts bend,
speechless, cold this evening, carrying stars, moonlight,
farther down river, farther down. To where?

# THE SAME PRAYER

Before the tabernacle, I genuflected to the seen and unseen,
what existed and no longer existed, like my sister Louise:

*In Nomine Patris et Filii et Spiriti Sanctum.* Always in the first pews,
old Polish and Slavic women: *Mater doloris.* Their lives spent

forgetting and remembering icy winds, fields, hills of Eastern Europe,
always in black, dresses and babushkas, black shoes that crossed rivers,

black rosaries like ropes from which hung their prayers. Blessed
was *the fruit of thy womb*—these widows of steel and wood

shuffled into church, tireless and stooped. They had washed blood
from knives, feces from bodies, keened over expired hopes, dead sons

and daughters: *at bedsides stood the mournful Mother weeping.*
They gripped black missals, thick as phone books, bulging with holy cards.

After Mass, I'd see them in the bakery store, selecting each nickel,
each dime, from coin purses, buying one, maybe two, sweet kolaches.

,　,　,

In white surplice, black cassock, I rang bells, inhaled the incense
of the Old Testament curling out of censers, the clink of its chain, rosaries,

votive candles, cruets, thuribles, stoles, vestments. We genuflected,
signed the cross, sang, *Kyrie eleison, Christe eleison, Kyrie eleison,*

summoned the dove of the Holy Ghost from the tree, summoned God.
The chanting stirred the congregation, rustled clothes—all an incantation;

*send forth Thy light and Thy truth;* all calling God down to our prayer bushel,
in each one an apple rubbed, polished on the day's vestment, red as horizon.

,   ,   ,

I held the paten under chins, solemn faces, receiving the Body and Blood
of Christ on their tongues, thick, muscular tongues, like my father's.

I saw white-spotted tongues, parched, blotchy tongues, twitching,
wagging, scolding tongues; tongues that reeked, tongues with cold sores,

bloated with gossip, sweet pink tongues of pretty girls. Back at the altar,
the conclusion: *Dominus vobiscum. Et cum spiritu tuo.* We were saved,

but would need saving many times, to recite the same prayer only changing
names from Aunt Marie to Uncle Louis, from my sister Louise to my brother

Tim, deranged by what he saw, did, in Vietnam, names for one bruised face
after another. How many times we'd beat our chests for sins that were not sins,

but were like shoes that gripped, created friction for the soul to move forward.
Without sin, we couldn't walk, recognize pain in each other, forgive ourselves,

anyone. Yes, we had harmed each other, betrayed loved ones. Some robbed,
beat wives, and wives would beat children; and so on until the sky itself

broke down like cardboard from weeping and crumbled:
*mea culpa, mea culpa, mea maxima culpa.*

# It's Not Music the Crow Plays

At night, when I'm trying to sleep,
a crow roosting in a nearby tree
raises its dark wings, lifts off a branch,

and lands on the keyboard
of a piano abandoned in the field.
With its beak, the crow strikes

keys at random, all night,
as if demanding I sit at the window
and listen. Once I aimed a .22

out the window and squeezed the trigger
into darkness. I want snow
like a white sheet to cover the piano

the way a mourner will cover
a mirror to forget. Once I dreamed
of a red scarf, floating in midair,

and I woke, reaching to the sky
of the dream, trying to pull
the scarf into this world.

A voice in my hospital room
said, "let go," but it was only the black
crow pecking at the keyboard.

My visitors say give it time,
the crow will tire,
another bird will come.

# MERCY

This is how the day begins:

opening my journal like one opens
the door to church for salvation.

Only ink, paper, loop and curl of letters
can absolve me of losses and trespasses.

To write as directly as I made the sign
of the cross as an altar boy—*In Nomine Patris*

*et Filii et Spiriti Sanctum*—on brow, heart,
and shoulders, marking my body as the lintel

and doorposts were marked in Egypt to save those
huddled inside. But how many times must I die?

Have amen pronounced over my soul?
Holy water of last rites sprinkled over my chest?

I lift off the hospital bed like a bird from a branch,
the bedsheet a cloud over the earth, as I flutter up

to make peace with the dead. But I return
to the living alongside my bed, and keep returning.

After losing love, I found love revised. What words
remain? Does a sentence surge like a river

into the afterlife? I won't argue whether God is
or is not, only that the heart, finding no expression,

depends on the mercy of language, syllables
of forgiveness, a pen to rub a word across flint,

to spark and light candles in a dark church.

# WHITE POINT, NOVA SCOTIA

This is the last. The end of color. Tonight,
after hearing frost warnings, I snip flowers,
make bouquets, bring them into the house
to die. One vase on a kitchen table, subject
for a still-life, lovely for everyone to see—
red petals falling onto the glass butter dish.
Remember it? And the flat white stone
we dug from the soil? Last month, I traveled
to White Point, Nova Scotia, as far
from the loneliness of our Midwest garden
as I could, flung our stone into the crash and spume,
white into white, into black undertow like soil.
I slumped on the grassy cliff. While I napped,
maybe a speckled gull alighted on my chest,
pecked at my heart, then flew up with my grief.
No, it was God lifting you out of my heart
because I could not. I don't blame you
for wanting distraction—at the window, waving to me,
while having lunch with him. You were learning
new words to describe me: *fish-in-the-sea, long ago,
once!* And I'm learning the names of our failure—
geranium, sunflower, magnolia, azalea.

# A Violet

At dusk, on the train, the fourteen-year-old boy leans across the aisle
to the woman wearing a straw hat with a blue violet, who sees in his brown eyes
a dream, and she, too, leans forward, smells childhood fresh in his hair.
She reaches across, touches his arm the way she once touched her husband's.
"I'm so sorry," she says, and feels a bird fluttering in her heart, singing plaintively.
She tries to imagine her own parents dying in a car accident on an icy road
in Ohio, the car spinning in circles for years later in her nightmares,
just like the boy is telling her, how sleep is more haunting than life,
how a toothless aunt with bifocals sends him away to a Catholic
military boarding school in New York. He tells every woman he meets
on the train this story, and on some days the aunt becomes an uncle
who drinks Jack Daniels. And every woman leans across the aisle,
touches his arm, like the woman with the violet, who later, when the sun
leaves and darkens the train car, scoots across the aisle to sit with him,
to talk, and let him pretend to sleep against her breasts,
touched by the boy she longs for.

# PLEASE NOTE

*Lentils are a natural product of the earth;*
*carefully sort out any foreign substance,*
*small stones, particles of soil, or metal.*

While rinsing the lentils,
I spot a pebble among the seeds
in the colander, the size of the one
my daughter swallowed at the lakeshore
when she was a year old. I found it
in her diaper, and rinsed and saved the stone
in a jar at home. I don't know why,
maybe because someday she might want
to see for herself why I worried.
Now at the kitchen sink,
I put this one from the colander
on my tongue, press it against
the roof of my mouth, click it
against my teeth, taste it
as she did hers when everything smooth
and cool on earth that summer day
at the lake was delicious, those days
when she had both her mother and me.

# Lilacs Scent Our Exile

Twenty years with the same photographs
of love and loss on the mantel. The Midwest sun,
centuries old, warps the lead glass; the house
sways in hellish winds; the limestone porch leans

and aches. I hear floorboards praying under my feet.
Memories clang, lights flicker a warning: the book
I read and love—it too—will end. In the evening,
the Mississippi sputters into my bathtub, large enough

for pain to stretch out. One night I found my house
emptied. A suicidal wind rushed the stairs. The river
poured through plaster, flooded rooms. The stink of water
rose to the second floor. Later, I swept out carp, beer cans,

condoms, film. Some nights, around the dining room table,
I stack books on each chair to take the place of guests.
At the table, Whitman, D. H. Lawrence, Neruda, and Amichai.
I serve pot roast with carrots, potatoes, onions, garlic.

Today, like every Saturday afternoon in May, St. Paulites
sweep out despair, paint the sky, hang dreams on clotheslines,
nail beams pried loose by the storm threatening everyone
in time. We garden or die. Lilacs scent

our loneliness and our exile from God. Yard sales advertise
what our children and lovers leave behind. A summer night
inevitably comes when we're convinced by candles
how easy life is, until voices bellow and weep outside.

One berates the other. We've heard this before.
We can't save the woman from his hand, if he lifts it.
*Stop. Go home,* we shout. From the street, he looks up
at my bedroom window, glowers at me, because my voice

reminds him of love, and he hates me for it, as if
my words mean I haven't ever fought a war like his.

# Blue Strawberry

I leave my friends in the theater, consult the sky,
and listen for the wind's advice. Cigarette smoke
whirls down the street into congested city lungs.
I hope someone passing or the stars will signal:
*No, don't call her,* or like the Leonid meteor last week,
spark an unequivocal *yes* across dark exhaust.
I can't recall her number, but know it resides deeper,
like the sliver from a wooden rake handle lodged
for months, maybe longer, until slipping out.
Memories lie on the tongue's taste buds or engorge
the cock; calcify in the skeleton of my hand that reaches
through summer morning air to her breasts as she sleeps.

Back inside, I drop coins in the pay phone,
wait for memory's blood to rush my fingertip,
start an instinctive electronic dance learned long ago
when calling her on a Sunday afternoon to bring a dress
for her to wear in the morning. If she answers,
I'll listen: *hello, hello,* until she's almost pleading,
*hellooo.* Half-suspecting, she might whisper, *Richard.*

A recording announces her number disconnected.
I picture her apartment: lights off, doors locked, the couch
where we fell asleep gone, along with the painting I hate,
and she lying now somewhere on a new sofa. I hang up.
Say nothing to my friends when the movie lets out
about how the body shelters memory, a phone number,
tingling like poblano on the tongue, indelible
on the soft flesh as the tattoo of a blue strawberry.

# In Defense of Kneeling

In my bedroom, a candle. I sip words from a book
like warm milk for an insomniac. Surely prayers
said in bed are no less as consciousness flickers.

If Kings David and Solomon, slaughtering tens of thousands
in every battle, commanding six hundred wives, three hundred
concubines, kneeled, can't I? Though never toppling Goliath,

I've seen and battled my own enemy-face. So I kneel
with the boy I was whose prayers were buoys for his sister
in a sea of tumors; I kneel with my father, the grief

of his dead daughters thick as ligaments in his knees;
I kneel with every Slavic and Polish man in steel mills,
tool and die shops on East 93rd Street. When night

crawled into their homes, they humbled their bodies.
Kneeling was like slipping into luminous bathwater;
they lathered their hearts, scrubbed them clean of guilt,

and soaked in gratitude for their wives faithful to impossible
hours. Doubt can't extinguish every candle flame,
any more than daylight can dispel every shadow.

Faith shines on Monday; faithlessness clouds Tuesday.
I salute the flags of disbelief, unfurling debris, regrets, and losses,
all shredded by wind. What I failed at or succeeded in doing

today my hands have forgotten; folded now on my lap
they're grateful to exist at this address and none other.
I can't distinguish now which is more silent and dark,

more still, the room or myself.

# BECOMING A CARNIVORE

This afternoon, a woman at lunch said you're now eating—
after twenty years of salads, tofu, soy, organic vegetables,
nuts, bran muffins, and fruits—
                    MEAT!

Holy Cow! What sudden impulse sunk your smile
into flesh? Low iron? A hunger for muscle and bulk,
breasts, and hips? What growled in your belly?

I can picture the dinner scene, the man you had over
the night you decided, secretly, to become a carnivore;
how at the table he sensed your immense craving,
perhaps mistaking it for him; how the wine glass reflected
your desire for meat: liver, calf tongue, bull testicles, breast,
pork chops, penis broiled, seasoned with testosterone.
The juice, your mouth open!

Forgive my slathering. My hormones sizzle.
Don't get me wrong. I still lust after you,
brood, long to tangle my tongue in your hair.

How delicious it must have been to teeter above
this strange craving for gristle and fat, as if it were an abyss;
how you must have salivated, licked your fingers,
grabbed the table edge, sides of your chair, before surrendering
to something so alien, prohibited, then steadied yourself,
with your knife and fork to masticate—fearlessly.

(Did he carve, did you study the knife in his hand,
back and forth in a familiar motion, each slice falling
like pink petals? O how the smell of rump roast
in the oven heats the body.)

There I go again.

When we ate together, you fed a different hunger.
You'd rub water spots off your fork or spoon,
carefully lift every vegetarian morsel, scrubbed and rinsed,
into your mouth. Your tongue articulated each bite
like a stubborn syllable of a foreign language.

Eat heartily, my sweetheart.

Buy steak, chicken, pork, sizzle bacon in the morning;
sink your teeth into fat. Doors to a delicious world
swing open for you: Reubens, hot dogs, sweetbread, hot pastrami
on caraway rye, pigeon, turkey, salami, liver. Let the smell
of pot roast excite that woman you starved and fit
into every tight short skirt, the woman whose thighs and arms
you scratched. Smear the juice over your tongue.
Here's a plate of steaming roast beef, gravy erupting
from a volcano of mashed potatoes, and you—
protein-charged, nutrient-powered, ready.

Damn. Someone inside me is slapping his thigh,
kicking his feet. My belly jiggles.

Sorry.

Honestly. After you left, I lived as a cloven-footed beast
in the forest, chewed leaves, roots, mushrooms, stones.
Darkness circled my fire, howled until who I was
flickered, digested by the cinders.
You were always Grade A, U.S.-inspected choice cut, most
succulent, shockingly red, most tender,
each nibble terrifying.

# Love Letter to Lucifer

I have read that one can advance
the cause of evil by convincing people

you exist only as a cartoon to doodle
in notebooks—tail, horns, cloven feet, pitchfork.

But the child in me believes differently
and asks you for a favor: *take her down*

*into your underworld.* Not forever, but long enough.
Keep her tight to the furnace, stoked by the damned,

so the flames lick her heels. Let not a man
be in sight on whose shoulders she might stand

or be cooled by his tongue. Ignore her perfumed cries,
but don't scar her. Singe her soles, so she might always

feel grief as she walks later on the surface
among those for whom suffering is only an itch.

Don't let her escape the fire by taking the hand
of someone new. Instead let her reach into smoke.

Tattoo a snake curling up her leg, its tongue
a warning for anyone who might come too close.

Perhaps my wishing you upon her only proves
the power of resentment, not of evil, and that I'm not

among the poor who will inherit the earth.

# The Blossom and the Coffin

1.

I could be you wincing
at the sun, pulling the visor
down, and tuning the radio.
How often your stubby thumb
and finger adjusted, like I do now,
the treble, resonating with memory.

The speakers at your farmhouse
have their mouths wide open
on your front porch:

Liszt is playing Saint Francis
in a concert hall, or does the piano
play out in the pasture
where music fills the alfalfa field,
and you walk in rippling purple flowers?
A crescendo of wind ruffles
your long black hair.
The cows follow, double bass
in the moonlight
as they cross into corn rows.
The stalks are clefs, marking
a path for your soul,
for the beasts.
We are stunned by the piano
that has brought us here,
playing now in the thirteenth century.
We live everywhere
all at once.

2.

As I drive past your house,
I see us up on the roof, hammers
hung from loops, and you, under the blue sky
challenging God
to a theological debate,
believing in music,
not prayer, while we shingle
to Beethoven on the radio
propped against the chimney.

You climb up here, a Jacob's ladder
in every rung, but still insist
paradise is held in your hand,
the grooved handle
to your hammer,
or smelled in lilac bushes,
heard when Chagall plays
a violin in his bathtub.

Here, at the roof's peak,
you say a man only needs to stand
to touch the sky, and see
there's no afterlife.
Joy's a plum tree in the yard,
fuchsia blossoms on earth.

3.

This pine tree I drive past
every Tuesday morning could be the one
in Montana along the Bitterroot River
when our twenty-year-old bodies
drank from the rivers
of the Rockies.

Ponderosa, you said.
And there, too, you pointed,
calling the crocus a haiku, the first
wildflower that spring.

I may still have years to walk
the trail into Patti Canyon
before I understand that moment
when my eyes close, done with living.
But you know what it's like
to be a child again, swinging
on vines, bending the tree's bough,

and at the same time letting go
of candlelight, tender flowers
that blossomed through your life.
In one glance, you see how
the blossom and the coffin
come from the same tree.

# INTO THE WILD

*We must take the feeling of being at home into exile.*
—Simone Weil

I want to swing open shutters to terraced groves,
olive trees, mountains and sea, or a pasture

where my fears lie down like a flock of sheep.
Instead, memories like laundry drape the railing.

Sleeves and shirttails drip with grief. Out there,
a distant hill, a slope of longing, and birds call.

I can't say what I long for. Starlight over Wolf Point,
Montana? Her? Words, perhaps? But none are large

enough, like yearning, to circle an entire life. When
did silence begin stealing words from my tongue?

When did I start revising my instincts, teaching
my emotions to enunciate like a gentleman?

My mistakes trigger no catastrophe or crime.
They're common as gravel inside shoes. Still, I'm tired

of wallets, ironing shirts, tired of every street,
every familiar branch, every storefront; I cannot get lost.

Give me one hour without memory of where I live,
who I am—a convict at the window scheming

to break out into the wild. O the self! I've educated him,
paid for his therapy, taught him to read maps of the heart,

purchased tickets for Athens, Paris, Rome, and Zurich
to expand his meditation on earth and sky,

but still he can ferret out only half-solutions, glimpses,
fragments, a coastline, never the entire sea, the good sense

of moonlight. Shackled to a name, a personality, I may
break out some night, lope like a collie across the field

to a fence, and bark at something beyond, a dark sentience.
Once or twice, I found on the other side an immensity

of wildflowers, pervasive smells, immeasurable sky, the self
dissolved into river and trees. What happened? At home,

I stand at the window, my back to oak furniture, listening
for a faraway voice on the front porch calling me at dusk.

Longing for leaves flushing a tree red, an end to the wandering
of desire, for a bridge to cross where the river below speaks

of a liquid joy. I am there, here, all at once. To be in one place,
though home is nowhere, and I go on knocking, one door

after another, knocking, waiting to be welcomed back.

# OUR USUAL PLACE IN THE UNIVERSE

Whatever we see at our usual place in the universe
on Saturday mornings, walking around Lake of the Isles,

or later in the evening, turning a page of a book;
whatever we say at Brenda's Cafe, with your wife

and friends, eating rainbow trout or salmon, where the clang
of fork and knife on porcelain nourishes a philosophy;

whatever we do, even suffering our bodies, endures
for only a wink before disappearing into specks of memory

the wind blows out the door of existence. Every morsel
of food, spice, and flavor as we are tasting them

scatter like leaves over an edge, a cliff. O to sip
black coffee forever. The cup warming my hands

for eternity. But always the coffee chills; the cup left
on the sink with dishes. Smells and sounds forgotten

as soon as I rise from the table or return to bed.
I could sleep, if my body didn't insist on tossing,

turning toward the window where I don't exist. Something's
true and enduring out there. Though we don't know what,

we live our lives elsewhere, asking, desiring, praying
for a fleshy heaven on earth, smells of sweat, something

to redeem all this creaking and cawing. It's no blessing
to desire to be a lake in which the heavens and stars

burn at night. But nothing else suffices. This explains
why rain keeps falling, gently, on the roofs of our stanzas.

One is no sooner written when it disappears from the desk
and day, leaving us longing, writing another, another,

because there's a place pure and lasting. Only I'm too flawed
to live there; every page too small to contain it. *All language*

*is a longing for home.* Though each word written is erased
by the wind, I keep opening my journal to bring heaven down,

opening a window onto this place as I revise and revise until
what I can't say is as clear as a painting of the sun setting,

each brush stroke holding dusk on the sprawling canvas
as light pulls away from the earth, and the dark holds sway.

## II

## TWO BODIES

*Strange indeed that illness has not taken its place with love and battle and jealousy among the prime themes of literature.*

VIRGINIA WOOLF

*Illness is the doctor to whom we pay most heed; to kindness, to knowledge we make promise only; pain we obey.*

MARCEL PROUST

# A Crack in the Dark

The nurse enters my room after midnight,
The soiled bandages she lifts out of my belly
smell like loneliness. Her other hand
rests on my chest, over my heart—all I need
to hold back the fear of the clock's second hand
circling like a line of radar. *Cold?*
I don't answer, but look out the window
into another century, while she talks about a patient,
a man much like me, only he believes his heart
was stolen during surgery, put in a hatbox,
sold on the black market. It leaves a hole in his chest.
The wind trapped inside howls. I understand.
One night, the man sleeps under his hospital bed,
believing nightmares coil in a nest on his mattress.
When she slides underneath to talk with him, he tells her
there are stranger things waiting for her, too, someday.
She can do nothing to keep him from dying.
Nothing, she says. Nothing any of us can do
for our broken bodies but suffer them. She touches
my brow, rubs her hand through my hair,
as she would other nights thereafter. She leaves
the door partially open, just enough for light
to open a crack in the dark; then she's gone.

# The Plum

1.

Thirty-five years ago
in Grandpa's backyard, I heard a snap,
saw a plum float in midair,
neither rising nor falling,
suspended between life
and decay.

Only after the plum fell
did I hear the voices
of life and death arguing.
The decision was in my hands:
to eat the fruit or let it rot.

Mother, you said: *Let God decide,*
but I was no more certain
than now, holding your hand,
your skin bruised,
soft and purple.

2.

After your stroke, a wheelchair
and shawl of sorrow, you curl your lip,
an old woman who has seen
enough. One side of your face
droops like wax, your tongue
tangles words.

How am I to know
what your finger means,
pointing to the respirator
and tubes, branches
your life hangs from,
feeding you oxygen and sap
through a vein? I will not consent
to watch you fall in slow motion,
pulse fading to a final bleep.

3.

Having closed your eyes,
you are in a place called
Nowhere, while across the street
I order black coffee,
clang my spoon among the living.
Cigarette ash falls
in my lap while I practice
reading obituaries,
block after block of fine print
that causes me no grief.

The bell above the door rings
nameless comings and goings
amid smells of grease and perfume.
But look! The rain outside
has moved in and clouds squeeze
under the restaurant's door
like vapors from a gas bomb.
Thunder shakes the tables,
the chairs and wall clock.
Lightbulbs pop! Our faces darken!
Silverware sparks with electricity.

We're carrying the storm
in our bodies! How wrong I was
to think that Nowhere would be safer
than the world.

4.

The phone rings at 7:00 a.m.
No choice now but to disconnect you
from life. A priest blesses your last
voyage, and we must pick a dress
for you one last time.

O Mother! Hesitate
before walking into the light
where all our deaths and losses
greet you, or just set a ladybug
on my sleeve, creak a rafter
in the house, let your shadow,
you have no use for now,
fall over me.

5.

I thought I knew where I was.
At home, staring
at the bedroom ceiling,
but I don't hear anything,
not even the familiar
whir of the fan,
drip of water.
I could be lying
under a gray sky

in a cornfield
or under a barren tree
alongside a road.
What happened
to the voices
mumbling nonsense all day
in my head, nonsense
I'm used to?
When I open my eyes,
I won't even recognize
who I am,
who owns these hands,
nor the name of this road.
All the maps
that pretend to chart
the landscape of grief
can't explain the silence
in the tops of the trees,
the dead leaves,
motionless air,
the slope of ground
down from your grave.
I can only drape an old coat
over my body,
pray someone will drive by,
recognize his own grief in me,
and tell me how to get from here
back to my bed,
the sunlight on your quilt.

6.

My daughter, Rosie, steps out
from behind me and stands
next to the bed,
wary of the purple bruises,
skin punctured with needles,
tubes down your throat,
nose, veins. She slips her hand
into yours, Mother. I step back,
the image of two namesakes,
two Roses, holding each other,
burns into my skin.
So when I speak of you
I can say, "Look,
I have this picture."
When we leave intensive care,
my daughter tugs on my sleeve
to show me how your fingers
lifted from the bedsheet,
curled a final good-bye.

Now I see. These words
aren't for my eight-year-old
to remember thirty years from now,
but for my future,
where I will go on,
never able to let go of you
or hold you close enough,
like that plum long ago,
neither rising nor falling.

# A BLOOD RACE

The nurse explains that the vein's diameter
and how hydrated we are

determines the speed of blood flow.
I propose twisting the needle like an awl

to open the vein wider, and she laughs,
swabs Mercurochrome, pokes our arms,

and clocks our race to fill the pint.
At breakneck speed, mine surges like rapids

in the Colorado River, but can't catch yours,
the winner, in six and one-half minutes.

Later at the refreshment table, dizzy,
we drink our obligatory glass of water,

orange juice, eat chocolate chip cookies.
We leave with our pockets bulging with apples,

not knowing then the meaning of HTVL cells,
specter of leukemia. I miss you today,

six months later, on the other angled gurney.
The cookies aren't tasty. It isn't funny.

# PHILOCTETES

For nine years, since Odysseus abandoned me
here to Lemnos, the ulcer from the snake bite
oozes foul-smelling green, making animals growl,
birds attack. I bark, crawl back to my cave,
drag the festering foot, blood-stained rags,
behind me. If only I had a sword

to chop it off.

Yes, I was banished from others; *and*
from the man I once was. A double sentence!
Fortunately, pain consumes memory.
I no longer recall life without it.

Now even the wind mistreats me,
burns inside the wound. Had my wound come from war
it would honor instead of disgrace me.

I have seen his ship pass near. The cowards!
It is not I, but the wound they exile.
Someday my scream will fill their mouths,
disturb their dreams. When awake, they will not
speak of what they heard. No one
exiles sorrow from his life.
We're measured heroes by what
we shout and endure,
not by what we deny.

# RIGHT THERE

Unlike the medics, I didn't notice
his lips blue as berries,
only the one eye, magnified
by a single lens of his bifocals

knocked half off his face.
That eye stared up at the ceiling
as if fixed upon a vision.
I looked up to see for myself.

The plumber lay on the floor
with his wrench still clamped
to the pipe under the sink,
as if waiting for his hand

to lift off his chest and grip it
the way he gripped his heart.
I had shuffled into the kitchen
but the silence, the hiss

of the kettle, his legs motionless
across the linoleum alarmed me.
Was he joking? *Come on.*
*What are you doing?* I asked.

Then I tapped his boot, stooped,
grabbed his ankles to pull him out.
Though months have passed,
that eye behind the lens

will open in a nightmare,
or when I'm buttering toast
at the table. I may look
again at the ceiling or cock

my head under the sink to inspect
the pipes because it happened
right there, in the curve
of the trap, in the gleam of steel,

in the jaw of the wrench.

# THE HUMAN PINCUSHION

Quiet and still, I gaze out a window as Father
removes the lathing hatchet lodged in my skull.

I'm seven. He calls me *courageous, a good soldier.*
And the afternoon I shoot my own finger with a .22,

he says, *Brave men bear pain.* I can't imagine
what he means. Mother's look often puzzles me.

Once, practicing piano, I bang my face in frustration
on the keyboard. She stares, as if my broken nose

were a monster's twisted snout. Why do others, too, stare
and gasp in parlors when I tug my lip forward, insert a hat pin

through it? To me, it's child's play to pierce each finger
with a pin, flash them like Gothic jewelry. I'm surprised

by those who shout when they prick their fingers. What,
I've asked, is pain? I try to understand, study their faces

and incredulous eyes for a clue, but I possess no genetic code
for pain, no fear in my own flesh, bones, joints, or teeth.

I don't itch or cry, can't be punished by man or God. Some say
immunity is wasted on me, because I have no idea of what I'm

spared. I should be sentenced to observe the dying in hospitals.
I've tried a normal life, playing clarinet for the U.S.

Marine Corps Band, working as a chauffeur, a ticket man
in a theater, until lured by money to vaudeville—

every evening at eight, matinees at two. Bare-chested, I invite
the audience onstage to push pins up to their heads

into my chest, fingers, soft flesh under my arms—
fifty or sixty pins at a time. *The Human Pincushion.*

I plan my own crucifixion—hawked as the Greatest Spectacle
on Earth. Not one seat in the house is empty. Never

have so many come to see a man die. The cross is hauled
onstage, and I lie down as if it were a divan. Lights dim,

drums roll, and my assistant hammers the first spike.
It must be the sound, steel against steel, or the squirt

of blood, that makes the audience panic and race out.
Fearing people might be trampled to death, we cancel

my performance. I'm disappointed. They know
I don't have to suffer to be redeemed.

I promise a painless crucifixion.

# FALLING

Only a week out of the hospital,
I hear my six-year-old cry,
fall from the top of the stairs,
and my quick start from the kitchen
knocks over a chair. Suddenly
we're each falling into our shadows.
I'm on the floor wiping blood
from my mouth, feeling my broken ribs
when sound rushes back into my ears.
*Daddy, Daddy,* she cries,
and I want to shout *Rosie, Rosie,*
the two of us calling out
through the terror of falling alone.
Though I can't move, my voice
tries to sound like Father,
calling her to this body
she couldn't imagine falling.
When her black shoes shuffle
into the room, the phone rings.
She turns away to answer it,
and I think she's handling this well,
though she has to point down
at me to describe how far
I've fallen, how tall she is.

# DYNAMITE

Inning after inning, it seems like the ball
has to squeeze through air molecules bloated
with humidity to arc over the left field fence.
During the seventh inning of the St. Paul Saints game
Dynamite Lady, wearing a helmet, red, white, and blue cape
and swimsuit crouches inside a box
at home plate jerry-rigged with explosives.
The bomb is no joke! The box
splinters, smoke swirls like deadly fog
on the ground where she lies motionless,
facedown, and that is when I remember
your son, his suicide, how you find him.
His death is an implosion no one hears.
Surely, something as solid as a bat remains broken
inside you. Lying on the ground, Dynamite Lady
pretends to be dead like we pretend sometimes
to be alive. And when her dog, Sparky, waddles
onto the field from the dugout to revive her
with his tongue, we clap, willing to accept
a happy ending. The baseballs go on rocketing
through blue sky, scooting under legs,
and I become strangely happy. I cheer
with the crowd when the freight train
passes from behind the center field fence
and those billboards that announce wonderful things
none of us need. We pump our arms to signal
the conductor that today no one suffers here.
He seems convinced, toots the train's horn,
long and hard, long and hard.

# ANATOMICAL WONDERS IN GIBSONTON, FLORIDA

Across the bridge over the Alafia River, Half-Girl owns a bait and tackle shop. She swings her torso between her arms, crosses the floor on her hands. Will I help navigate her wheelchair? Ask about the nine-foot giant, her deceased husband, and their life as the World's Strangest Couple?

Sideshow freaks expect cameras and journalists, not a middle-age poet in jeans, carrying a backpack, without press credentials and camera crew. As I drive past palm trees, Turbo Marine, Adult Mobile Park, and green February grass like an apron around the waist of Tampa After Dark video store, I wonder what will Half-Girl and I talk about?

The gravel crunches under the tires, and when my car door slams shut, I think, *of course.*

Walking to the gas station's bathroom to empty my ostomy, I realize I've been driving this road for years. Ever since I left the hospital and the surgeries that cut, looped, and finally snipped and threaded bowel into my own Anatomical Wonder, the sensational see-it-to-believe-it sight on my abdomen. Coming here to interview Poobah the Dwarf, Half-Girl, Lobster Boy, and the Human Blockhead isn't out of my way at all.

# MARY

Your name is blessed
on my lips like Mary,
Mother of God, Mary
Magdalene. Your name,
called across the fields
of Czechoslovakia,
scrubs, irons, and cooks
in the homes of foundry
and steel workers.
Mary, maid to my mother's
eight children, you are Martha
of the New Testament,
your hips sway all morning
at the ironing board
while the steam whistles
nursery rhymes.
I fold handkerchiefs
into clouds for you,
the towels are capes
that let me fly,
the clothes basket
a wicker boat
you help me row.
Mary, you're Merlin
making wooden spoons clap
and dance in bowls,
inspiring dough to dream
of cinnamon and sugar,
teaching my fingers obedience
as I tie your apron's bow

or the babushka
under your chin.
Mary, I'm always a boy
in your lap, lying my head
on your breasts
where the hooves of a horse
trot in your chest
and I fall asleep
in a meadow.
Mary, Angel of Mercy
to my dying sister,
Moth of Light
and Scrubber of Floors,
a Marmalade Queen,
Mermaid in the sea
of our family,
I carry your name
in my blood. Milkovich,
I call your name
when I am drowning
in a wave of fever,
and you're the warm tea,
the white sheet tucked
under the sick boy,
inhaling your breath
until there's nothing
left of you. All
the children in Ohio
you feed and nurture
become young men and women
who lift your casket.
It's your name we chant.
Your name, Mary,
Mary Milkovich.

# Arse Poetic: A Defense

True! I take syllables seriously.
Each stanza corrals horses named IV,
Dr. Merlin, Scrub Nurse, Demerol & Colon.
So? What are your *Equidae* named:
Sweet Pea, Chocolate, Sugar Pie?

You say lethal mushrooms grow on my poems.
Readers need flashlights, miner's hats, oxygen
& cables to find their way. No one can bear
such pain. "More distance," you say,
"from the man in the hospital bed.
Who can bear the smell?"

Listen. I walked over broken glass into the afterlife.
A surgical table smeared with blood (sorry)
became a raft I sailed to the Town of Deepest Appreciation.
Words seeded with pain sprouted into green trees, flowers.
Some words had no objective correlative:
sigmoidal, ileostomy, ileanal.

Excuse me! If a metaphor compared me
to a gorilla in the rain forest, I'd scratch my tits, fart,
and grunt. No one would think me crude.
Or in a zoo, I'd pound my chest, slam myself
against Plexiglas, over and over. Everyone
would shudder, stand back, knowing
some things aren't funny.

Here are my reasons: blue sky, chimney smoke, and wisps.
What more do you want? Teacups speaking
on saucers, roses nodding their heads
when you pass? They only make the wind snore.
No. The body is a temple in ruins.

My worldview reads like this:
I have crawled into a cave using a lantern
called morphine, laid hopeless on a dirt floor.
Even that mattered. Do you need proof?
Here I am.

# The Submarine

In prison, inmates spoke of it,
but I couldn't imagine myself a submarine,
until stripped, my hands tied behind my back,
feet roped together. I was lifted into a tub
of foul-smelling water. Soldiers forced me
under. I fought and splashed until someone
stomped on my chest, dancing. His boots
broke ribs. The water I swallowed
filled my lungs, and all the while a bell,
like the one that clanged on Sundays at my church,
rang in my ears until I died. I was certain.
The pain left, and a single star lit the entire sky.
Suddenly, a hand reached into my universe,
yanked me out—a soldier pounded my chest
with his fist. Water squirted from my mouth.
They questioned me. My answers meant nothing.
They threw me back into the tub.

I couldn't believe a man could die more than once,
surface, plunge again, and return to language.

# THE ANATOMICAL WONDER PLAYS DEAD
# IN THE DOCTOR'S OFFICE

Not one empty chair in the waiting room. Eighty-two, the oldest
living sideshow performer, you grow impatient at the prospect of
paging through *Time* while pain radiates down your shoulder. As
Greta Garbo did in *Camille*, you lift your hand to your brow and
swoon, then slam yourself hard against the wood, the wall, onto the
floor.

"My God," a patient whispers. Your arm twists behind your back,
scapula dislocated, unfurling a shoulder blade like a broken wing
as if you had fallen out of the sky. No one plays dead better than
you. This time, it's easy. No one has asked you to dive headfirst into
a barrel of water, wrestle orangutans, swing from Roman rings, or
pound railroad spikes up your nose.

A medic sees only milky moonlight under your eyelids, then presses a
finger against your carotid, lays his head on your chest, as if listening
for the occlusion of gurgling blood. His hair smells like your son's.
And you remember that afternoon he stood against the target, an
altar, and he the sacrifice, while you threw knives between his legs,
around his young face like a glistening nimbus.

Days later, at the hospital, when a nurse leans over you in bed to
read *acute myocardial infarction* in your chart, you reach up to
touch her cheek, run your fingers through her thick black hair, and
nearly forget to pull the ace of spades out from behind her ear.

# WHITE

How many words are there for *white*?
Opal, alabaster, soul, clouds,

ivory, bones, virtue, eggshell;
yet nothing now needs a name

as I float away up into an alcove of white
brilliance, while Roseann reads aloud

at my bedside, and a milky stream
of light flows over my feet

and what must be floor, though nothing
squares off above or below. A single window

with its shade pulled appears,
and though I can't see the door

somewhere one swings open,
both ways, for me to enter or leave

the light. I can't explain how
I know the width and height

of my soul, atomized into purity,
but if I choose to stay,

the view outside the window
will be mine. When my fingertips

touch the shade, I materialize
in the hospital bed, knowing

what I have chosen. I try to lift
my hand, tied to the bed rail,

to interrupt her reading and say,
above the whir of the respirator,

*snow*, as if I were calling her
by one of her many names.

# THE DOUBLE

At the airport, the detector alarm sounds.

I lift my arms as the inspector passes a metal bar down my front,
then the back. How could he guess that I'm reconfigured
with wires, metal clips, adhesive. My other body
was created on a surgical table in Minnesota.

Being two is not a metaphor.
One body, disfigured and hidden, prefers the dark.
The other is here, the one everyone calls Richard.

An X-ray would let inspectors see shadows
where they shouldn't be: metal, plastic bags, absence.
I'm not surprised: matter conflicts with spirit.

They examine my passport, medical documentation.
He seems to understand and permits us both
to enter his country.

# BETTING ON AFTERNOON LIGHT

For luck, some knock on wood, toss salt, hoping
to nudge from the universe a random blessing.
I depend on the mercy of numbers. I note addresses,
count stars, trust the seventh hour of every day,
examine a cluster, say, my nurse's name,
Sharon. The six letters, my sixth hospital stay,
the six days God created the world, and me, the sixth
child in my family—all omens, synchronicity.
I gamble in a spiritual casino for grace
while shuffling down the hospital corridor
for surgical good fortune, the efficacy of a new pill.
I believe an unfathomable Mind intervenes
through algebraic formulas, dividing or multiplying
events. Like a mathematician, God answers prayers,
subtracting one life, adding others to compensate.
He blesses sevenfold, after taking everything.
In the Bible, someone's always counting cubits,
oxen, concubines. I love the number zero. In it
resides the moon, the sun, the day round as a clock.
Zero appears twice (also good) in my hospital phone number,
keeps me believing the random acts of unkindness,
accidents, and illnesses will be righted. True or not,
doesn't matter. I learn from illness nothing happens
when I expect it to. Sunlight slants in now
through the window at forty-five degrees, and my pain
subsides at 4:50 p.m. I know desperate men
seek signs they're not alone, not yet, help is coming.
Afternoon light through the window tells me so.

# Lazarus Comes Home

I am Lazarus in a new millennium. Called forth
from behind the closed door of my hospital room.

Infection courses through my blood.
My intestines perforate, drip into a visceral cave.

Out from surgical rooms, I'm called forth: *Lazarus*.
Then a chorus, *Lazarus*, in B-flat. Later, on the street,

I walk with a cane; crows in trees caw: *La za rus*,
each syllable accenting a life without morphine, blood,

and bandages. Sparrows with grass-thread stitch
my abdomen shut. When my sister dies

in the back room of the house, when Father is driven
in a hearse to the Promised Land, then Mother years later,

each time I'm called to my front door, to windows,
to see my neighbor's flower garden like none other.

On Saturday nights, I dress for salvation, make love
after midnight. I press my ear against her vagina;

a voice inside calls me to my birth: *O Lazarus*.
Have I not come forth each time? How many times

must I die? I argue with the darkness: *I'm tired. I'm not
for this life. There are better men. Let them bear witness.*

But the voice persists. I step back from the cliff. Or is it
a river I refuse to cross, until I'm rowed by friends

to the other side while half-conscious from an overdose
of despair? I don't know who brought me home, but I am,

by accident, destiny, or grace. I don't care what magic,
philosophy, or deity claims my life. I believe. I listen,

unwrap my bandages, stand naked in my room.
Now, it's enough to be called simply *Richarrrd*,

the way my mother used to call me home at sunset.
I open windows, boil water, slice strawberries.

Someone is calling. I pick up the phone: *Richard?*
My daughter shouts my name from upstairs;

and I answer, over and over, *I'm here.*

# THE TEACUP

After the hospital, forced
to study the intricacies
of snow crystals on the window,

I've come to look closely
at details, like the curve
of this blue teacup's handle,

how my finger hooks under my thumb,
lifting more than water, steam,
and rose hips, because at any moment

the phone could ring, or pain
like a rope suddenly knotted
and cinched inside my abdomen,

might scatter porcelain chips
across the floor. Now that's why
the cup on the saucer

is the first and last
in this house, on this earth,
the only cup that matters.

# THE IMMENSITY

*So we came forth, and once again beheld the stars.*
                                        —Dante


Strange how shameful sorrow feels.

As if it were not one of four pillars holding up the world,
but only a demon incinerating hope. Had I known
the infections and surgeries would leave me
with such ragged joy, inexplicable to myself,
at this hour of eternity where I am more,
I wouldn't have kicked the ambulance doors, but instead
endured the flesh longer like the weight of the sky,
always changing. Turn back the page, I'd never
choose pain, but when it shatters a window
(and it always will), I'd be more willing, game even,
to welcome the final cry and slash, knowing the heart,
when wrenched from its selvage, its place inside,
will seek to fill the eventual immensity.
Before they'd lift my body into bed, anesthetize it,
I'd pause, if possible, until the pain, more pressing,
more violent, more continuously present, breaks
the clench of my teeth, my resolve, and I'd swoon,
fall from that sky of immeasurable width and depth.
Picturing this fall is unbearable, unthinkable,
but trust me the fierce consciousness that's gained
consoles, like an angel unfolding its wings,
revealing, at last, its beautiful chest and torso.

## Two Bodies

Like me, you have two bodies.

One as beautiful as a Cuban sunset.
The other, birthed by surgeons and technology.
You explain the wire like a vein plugged to your spine,
traveling subcutaneously around your waist,
emitting electrical pulses that switches your bladder
on or off. *How fortunate.* Our bodies accept

metal and rubber, clamps and tubes, what we need to live.
All because of one evening in Detroit, 1990, when fog
pasted the seconds before the crash to memory.
Another 747 landing slices open the fuselage
of your plane from nose to tail with its wing,
making the sky the ceiling. Stars explode

like lightbulbs; the moon careens out of control.
Clouds of smoke begin to rain gas, and a meteor
rolls toward you, in slow motion, from the rear of the plane,
igniting passengers like candles in the aisle. It isn't God
that abandoned them to flames and spared you,
but a random bump and push

just when the emergency exit swings open,
and throws you clear of the wreckage. That's why
we're grateful now. Leave a hearty tip for the waitress.
And once outside you gesture to the sky, clouds;
curl your finger and punctuate the air, as if typing:
*Here! This is good! This is what I meant to write.*

# III

## PRAYERS OF THE PEN

*There is no beauty without the wound.*

# Prayers of the Pen

1.

Dip my pen in blue sky,
wise ink.
Free it from logic,
shackles of punctuation.

Bring my pen to Solomon.

2.

My pen seeks one prayer.

I walk Selby Avenue
to the Cathedral. Is not the intention
to pray better than any prayer
my pen could write, my mouth say?

What does the wind say to the man waiting for a bus?
What does the sky say to the woman stepping out her front door?
What does an iris say when it colors a memory?

Not a thousand words say so much.

I live half my life in silence.
So much seeks
*language as large*
*as longing.*

What does the sunflower say to my eyes?

3.

In my journal I seek
daily reconciliation.
But I fall asleep in a sentence.
Or chase after words
wearing nylons.

O God of the River
who sits on the rocks as I float by—

swimming, drowning, obedient.

4.

Lay one word, one smooth stone,
on my tongue.

Sustain me at your door.

My father taught me one
sure prayer: *help*.

5.

Your Word circles the whole;
but each one my pen writes
is amended with another, another.
We quarrel. I reproach it
for its limitations. In turn,
my pen argues, "I don't exist.
I only shape loops and curls.

What's missing is
missing in you."

Grant us peace.

6.

My pen is so stupid.
Forgive my pen its trespasses.
My pen lusts
for Amelia, Daphne, Susanne,
their legs and breasts.
My pen desires fame and fellowships.
Feels murderous.
It could not care less. Teach me
to endure its shortcomings patiently.

7.

Which street? I don't know
the direction or the difference
between virtue and vice—when
one leads to the other.

My pen inhales this morning's fog.

8.

My pen writes her name, the letters
uncurl, rise off the page like smoke.

Later, I walk down the street
without a button or thread from her dress,
a strand of her hair.

Some prayers require motion.

9.

In Santa Fe, the Prayer of the Staircase
is unsupported, with no center beam.
Not one single nail is needed
for ascension. Each step
rests on each step.

Its prayer

is measured, sawed, planed,
tongued, and grooved
to build purpose, endure.

Like hands that fold
blankets, discover the past
under beds, and give body
to prayer.

Every prayer must
kneel, swim, hold a pen,

begin in flesh.

10.

Start my pen on the right margin.
Move it left across a landscape
to a town where the moon is fearless,
where my pen eats apples instead of ashes,
an orange instead of dusk, blue sky
instead of memories. May it escape
mortal conclusions,

if only for this afternoon.

11.

My pen is exhausted.

I devote myself to things that die:
corks to empty bottles, a match that flares.
My two hands—ignorance and suffering—
hold prophesies of doom.
My poor shoes walk in only one direction.
What they don't know is immense.
I turn right when left is the truer path.
Why here? Bring me home.
Quickly.

12.

Today, my pen blesses
saplings, becomes honest,
and waters the garden.

Each shrub and iris of language
grows wild. The pen copies petals
of images, drawing life from life.

It kneels in the dirt,
bows before sunflowers,
praises a cardinal lifting into a sky
spreading over pages of history.

Bless the garden, blossoming
and wilting, seasons existing
for writing, for dying.

13.

My pen copies: *prayer preceded God...*
*created God,* and I kneel now
at the edge of a cliff, before a steep
darkness where every syllable matters.
Like my pen, I believe that the unwillingness to stay
quiet in our rooms causes unhappiness.
And the truest prayer is said
before we say it, before we tongue
our intention, at the moment
our minds turn north, *to what is.*

# IV

## TRUE NORTH

*You purchase pain with all that joy can give,*
*And die of nothing but a rage to live.*

# The Smell of Apples

*We do not remember days, we remember moments.*
                                        —Cesare Pavese


One summer day, sitting under an elm, I smell
baked apples and shudder. Over me, a leafy aperture
yawns benevolently. I fall slowly up into the tree,
overwhelmed by its branches and sweetness.
The green so palpable I reach into it, when the pressure
of a hand—how do I know?—holds me still. I enter
what is livid with green, alive, surrounding me with grass
and sky, though if direction exists it's boundless.
I become weightless; hear leaf brush against leaf;
and my fingers, knuckles, and skin, so tender
they don't seem to belong to my body, but another's.
I have never before touched bark or stem. It's more
than my body can stand, and I return to the man I am
leaning against the tree trunk, out of breath. Only now,
I understand how suddenly it happens. A smell of apples,
something thin as a shaving of wood, or the map of a leaf
becomes wide enough to let one into another world,
where space is an interior to something larger,
improbable, immense, and near at hand.

# A Horse Named Sex

She pictures sex as a merry-go-round:
horses trotting to organ music—all tethered
to a center around which they circle.

*It's a spiritual thing,* she says, that saddles
and domesticates the animal, otherwise
it would escape the corral, a bucking bronco of lust.
*Whoa,* I want to say, but she's from Venus
and hears carousel music, the flanks under her thighs,
while I hear jazz and saxophones groaning,
lifting and twisting the platform out of shape
until only the body is at the center, unsaddled,
galloping north and south, east and west.

Sex, my tongue says, has no center. What
we bring to love must first be lost in the wild
and only later, dizzy with the delight of stars,
we gaze like ancient astrologers on heavens,
connecting one star to another, tangled and curved,
until out of sparkling chaos, the universe
becomes our bodies, shaping constellations—
a horse we mount and ride into love.

# THE BATHTUB

A white wing of curtain unfurls in the breeze.
Near midnight, with a full moon,
we climb in the tub, push off shore. She captains
the porcelain boat to the Country of Wide Senses,
where rose oil welcomes, and Handel's water music plays.
Trumpets herald our coming down the river
with balanced cups of tea and lavender. She lifts
her feet onto my chest, and I wash them.
We lean back. The wind of our desire billows.

Once, in Greece, I saw ancient tubs
of clay and stone. Beached like whales,
tubs then were deep enough for a man to sink
below with fish and eels. Invented for royalty,
but loved more by the poor for whom dirt
is a second skin, those tubs soaked bones of grief,
but not ours, not now, not tonight.

I'm lucky. Having received last rites twice,
I can still crouch in a skiff of porcelain, sail
with a woman I love who recites Marvell and Yeats,
and stroke the tattoo of candlelight on her skin.
When I glance out the window under the sail of her back,
it's so easy. There, on the tablet of sky, another poem.

## ATLAS REVISITED

The old story starts with a handsome idea,
in front of the mirror. My hair
combed in a wave of thick desire.
I was Atlas, shouldering cities,
Hercules, battling for justice,
the first man on a great journey.

But flesh is gravity.
Peels away like bark.
Even the soul fails to shelter it.
A knife of sorrow slices it open.

I took the body's muscled nights for granted.
It's an old story, a youthful mistake.
I paid handsomely for it.

My dreams were left standing
like wooden, deserted shacks
on the edge of town. This was
a blessing.

Now an apple fits perfectly in my hand.
Now I salute young men who climb
and never tire of falling.
Now dust settles on the photograph
of who I was, and I put him on the mantel,
among my loved ones.
Now I'm happy for no reason.

# END OF SUMMER

Long ago, I left to comb the frontier for wild horses,
grizzlies, women with hair tangled under their arms,
men who polished spittoons. I hitchhiked
down roads of Ponderosa, honeysuckle, lilacs,
slept in a row of towering cornstalks.
I imagined every woman in love
with the flowers blooming in my footfall,
my philosophical brown eyes. A fabulous fire
consumed me, my secret life. The wind stayed ahead,
blew open tavern doors. I leaned against the bar,
guzzled, belched, passed out.

I walked west to keep the sun from setting
on my life. Decades later, when illness
twisted my intestines; when poverty looted
my wallet and hope; when the clock expired;
I surveyed the landscape and ruins. I admit:
I prayed, confessed to crimes I had not committed.
I hated what I saw, despised my own need to be
forgiven. I abandoned existential campfires,
pushed away jiggers of whiskey, pledged devotion
to my daughter, showed up at work, kept a calendar.

That young man stands now at my window.
Folds his arms across his chest, stares accusingly.
He's right. I'm surrendering, bone by bone,
tooth by tooth, mending clothes,
preparing for a far stranger journey.

# THE BODY REPROACHES THE SOUL

*And if the body were not the Soul, what is the Soul?*
                                    —Walt Whitman


Have you forgotten? I gave birth to you,
bound your wings to my shoulders. My flesh
created desire, the word More, your quest.

Inside muscles and neurons, you reside
not as prisoner, but as strength, energy.
On evenings, when my legs raced down corn rows,

pumped a swing into the crisp air, you named
the sensations—sweat, heart beating, taste of salt
on lips—heavenly. Then, you forgot. For years.

And imagined God bodiless and everywhere.
Now you seek to fly above the earth's density,
leave behind toenails, stubble, teeth, and escape

through some aperture in the sky. Why?
Here, we taste strawberries, mangoes, plums,
see orioles, smell peonies, dahlias, fuchsia.

Have you forgotten which came first:
the iris or beauty? The kiss or love?
My blood flows through your abstractions;

bones shelter them. Even in the afterlife,
the body's not excluded. It doesn't turn to ash
but reassembles, cell by cell. Then it stands

on tiptoe, picks peaches from a branch.
Don't panic. I'll carry you on my shoulders
into a garden; everyone we have loved will follow,

wearing the familiar flannel shirts, jeans,
lace collar. Dogs will bark, leaves will fall.
It will be a good day like any other.

# What the Hats Whisper

Nested in boxes, on shelves or hooks, forty-seven
in all. From catalogs, Saks on Fifth, Gantos,
the Lilletorget in Malmo, Sweden, London's Portobello

Road Market, or Ekotryck, Belgium. She's never
without one: a bubble pillbox, bowler, beret,
molded crowns or felts. Each hat a persona—

angled for audacity; a rim folded for reticence.
Each morning she must choose: ostrich feather,
buckram, fabric flower, or grosgrain ribbon?

Everyone has heard the hats—Cloche, Derby,
Tiara, Hood, Cowboy—talk about the smell of her hair,
her sensuous thoughts. Once I considered lifting

a baku straw, trying it on, but realized my thoughts
might frighten it. My poor bald head weeps.
The hats love her more than any poet ever will:

*Aren't we lucky to be this close,*
*to rise and fall with her every step.*

# PILGARLIC

Assume longing resides in the body.
Inside my head, almost bald, is a likely place.

Or in my colon, now a casualty.
In hands, in prayer.
In my feet, slogging through memory.
In my chest, a logical place for her.

In breath, cough, phlegm.

Or coded in a gene
passed from one generation to another, since Eden.
So it's Adam longing inside me.

Maybe longing resides outside.
In the eyes of passersby on Selby Avenue,
at Nina's Cafe where we sip longing,
dark roasted; or in the moon,
its face on a white pillow.

The sky? Perhaps. It pelts us with hail.

Maybe longing breathes in things themselves:
my mother's rosary, zippered in a black leather coin purse,
hollow bird bones, garden hoe, leaded window,
and when touched contaminates us with sweet poison.

Maybe yearning to run my fingers through her hair
produces a static, neurological paradox,
smoothing and shining the top of my head.

Assume I grow bald from all this longing.

# LAUGHING FALLS

1.

It took seven hours to lose our way.
We hiked up Mt. Yoho, Valley of Wonder
in Cree, over ridges and Pleistocene boulders
under which marmot lived; past eskers and Canadian
anemone, pearly everlasting, western paintbrushes,
purple asters and bunch berries; along the ice-line trail
marked with cairns, stones arranged for eternity;
glaciers which trickled into blue-green lakes
and waterfalls of ice cubes. We tired,
got separated from the others,
and missed the cutoff
down to Laughing Falls.
Lost.

2.

*Ryoooozooo! Ryoooozooo!*

3.

You must have worried. Had I broken a leg?
I could have stayed in the stratosphere,
among glaciers, surrendered to the wind, cold, and sun,
to the rock where we ate lunch earlier,
the ice of an emerald tarn where we swam,
to any one of the fields of alpine flowers
where only angels could sleep
without crushing the petals.

4.

How do you paint a mountain?
Lift this rock and glacier into a poem?

I kept looking back. Could we go deep enough
into the woods and forget our own names?

5.

Shadows moved among trees,
followed us close behind. I saw them.

Our guide had recommended we travel light,
but I had brought memories of the dead
in my wallet.

No wonder that climb was so steep. I sat and rested,
slipped off the backpack, and hoped
I was never found.

6.

*Come, come,* shouted Ryozo,
the first to greet us.

The waterfalls drummed the boulders
as rock wobbled under his feet. He inched
toward the hundred rainbows
inside the water spray. His wet shirt clung like skin.
I could see why, when he finally waved,
the falls were Laughing, made us exuberant.

When he opened his arms, the wind lifted
his hat, pitched it into the air.

*Yiiiieeeeeee!*

# Then Let Me Bring

At the gate, if we must bring one thing—
something wooden and contoured, an antique,
a collection of baseball cards, china doll,
a song we've composed and played on the violin—
to show Saint Peter, to convince him
we haven't wasted years on earth complaining
about the cold in winter, the heat in summer,
one thing that will astonish even the angels,
one shape that hasn't yet been conceived,
one word precipitated from the centrifuge
of our life, or even a somersault, a salute,
a handshake like no other that God has gripped,
then let me bring, not a poem, not my flute, not the box
of silver dollars my father left me so my hands
might feel the solid touch of money,
not even a photograph of my daughter to show the dead;
no, instead I will bring this velvet bag, unloosen
its string, lift out the orange, red, and yellow,
and begin tossing the balls into orbit like moons
in a path around my body, each one spinning,
showing God what my hands have learned
when they weren't clutching sorrow.

# ROSES AND THORNS, POTS AND PANS

Already my daughter's history is written. At seventeen,
she turns its pages back to photographs of her father, Caesar
of the Roman Empire, who once ruled her day.

Now I'm an archeological ruin, needing excavation.
She travels farther away from this house to her own roses,
thorns, pots and pans, a handsome gorilla she'll love,

civilize with fork and knife, make him do heart-work.
Her life widens like a tributary to the sea. Every day I pack
her suitcase: I fold patience like a blouse to wear

when clouds make the sun late arriving at her door,
a knife to separate good from evil, the Psalms, charm bracelet,
a ticket for a mule ride through Santorini, a chair

and open window for yearning. I lick travel stickers
on her suitcases: Destiny, Paris, Promised Land,
River Jordan, and Help, Iowa. She'll learn alchemy

in a hotel, and from so much travel, earn a Ph.D.
in the Cartography of Soul. I jerry-rig ropes for her
to lower herself into rivers where dreams flow safely back

to her bed. I pack toiletries: a hairbrush for when life
ravishes her, a razor for severing, a hand mirror for mortality lessons,
indulgent bath bubbles, whispering mist, soaps, but No Makeup.

She'll have to rely on her own beauty. Zippered inside a pouch
our front door key, a star from her bedroom ceiling.
I'm writing notes on the margins of her consciousness:

*Endure your shortcomings patiently, read, love the truth*
*even when it smells of garlic, keep no secrets the devil might love,*
*when the time comes, risk it all, fly,* and *the number twelve.*

She'll know its meaning. For the day she crosses a river and wishes
she hadn't, I remind her forgiveness will ferry her back.
And when my phone number is deleted from the White Pages

of this world to call me in the other. I'll rattle windows,
clang radiators, raise goose bumps on her skin until she's
convinced, and the door between us swings on its hinges.

# Shoelaces

They wind together like the forks
of a river. In peril, when knotted.

Feel no grief when broken.

We assign them purpose,
untie them from it every evening.

Like buttons, windows, salt,
they keep silent until forced
to speak in metaphors, yielding
to our intense need.

Poverty or pain
makes them seem perishable.
And after a long siege,
I leaned over a miracle
my fingers looped and tied into a bow.

When you can't say
*showgirls,* or have no desire
for show and tell,
look down and say it slowly:
*shoelaces, shoelaces.*

# Why a Poem Ends in Death

Every poem ends in death.
Every revelation brings death to what existed before it.
Every pen fills with rain to record afflictions
and can't imagine what lies ahead of its nib
as it journeys down the path of a sentence
to the end of ink. Inside the poem, the poet seeks
his own dissolution in the sky and grass. He's not
summoned out of the tomb, but *into it.*
To create sunlight where there is none.
He dies for this joy.

# TRUE NORTH

*After a first line by Robert Hass*


What August proposes in Banff is susurrus leaves;
Mount Rundle, wrapped in a scarf of cumulus clouds,
leans like a ladder against the sky for anyone
who wants to flee words like *telephone* and *doorbell*;
magpies in blue-black and white squawk on the lawn;
Ryozo paints in his studio this morning; Madeline, seventy-six,
ices her feet after hiking to Larch Valley; Judy writes
in a boat lifted off the forest floor on planks,
moored to the pines. She names each poem after an animal
to bring on board. The words themselves will billow,
she says, set the boat in motion. I believe her. It's easy to trust
this wind. Today everyone's employed by happiness:
the opera company rehearses; Diana prepares an exhibition.
Clouds prowl the base of the mountains.

Ryozo recites the names of the four peaks—
Bourgeau, Brett, Copper, Storm—that the nurse wrote down
for him on paper like a prescription; they might be antidotes
years from now, and I laboriously copy them. I must remember
the names of every wildflower, twists of the Bow River,
velvet antlers, gondola, and blue bike. It all matters.

We've worked so hard to get to this hour of our lives.
Hauling luggage, we've sat down on the edge of beds,
unfolded our marriages, deaths, and children like clothes.
We could put them in hotel drawers, small pillboxes,
even a container filled with holy water from Chimayo.

With so much, no wonder our bodies tire. Memory
is a steamer trunk. That's why we seek flotation
and light; why Ryozo and I now outside

stand back to back in the dark, under constellations,
stars snapped on the vest of night, and search the sky
for the North Star. *There?* he points. *No!* I say.
*Maybe there* ... And like a wheel, we turn round and round,
circling to see each other's heaven.

## Oil and Rags

I hung ropes from Truth Trees
to swing across the river, built bridges
with books, studied Gurdjieff and Eckhart
as if they were my boats, but the river
kept widening, deepening, a current
I couldn't hold.

Drugs and booze bought me courage and oars.
I lost both in the first rapids. I read
the *Awful Rowing Toward God,* held out my hand
for St. Christopher, but he forgot to score my ticket.
I would have paid handsomely for any woman

to ferry me. I even tried stripping down,
tearing my clothes into cords and strings
so I could parachute into paradise. My night
of oil and rags flowed longer than the Mississippi.

I always found myself nowhere I could name,
cracked in the head, thinking my body had failed me again,
but what of my soul? Could I lift it and give it back
to the body of the universe? Would there be time?

I still walk the riverbanks, searching the waters
for the shadow that steps faster than my feet.
God hides behind God. Now you see Him, now you don't.

Boats, bridges, freshwater mermaids, no matter.
Nothing gives up enough shimmer to steer by.
The will, the wanting, the pounding of the rudder

is of no avail when one tries to cross the river alone.
I should know. I'm back there and I'm here.

God, bring me to the headwaters that aren't divided
into two shores; where nothing is right or left,
east or west, and it makes no difference
from where all the rivers come....

# Notes

The quotes "all language is a longing for home" in the poem "Our Usual Place in the Universe" and "language as large as longing" in the poem "Prayers of the Pen" are from Rumi.

"The Human Pincushion" was a name commonly adopted by sideshow performers such as Edward Gibson, who had a congenital immunity to pain. He appeared with his doctor before the New York Neurological Society at the Academy of Medicine in 1932.

"The Submarine" is written after consideration of a letter written by a Portuguese torture victim to Amnesty International.

"Anatomical Wonders in Gibsonton, Florida" and "The Anatomical Wonder Plays Dead in the Doctor's Office" are in memory of Melvin Burkhart. I want to thank Joe Richmond for his referrals and his NPR broadcast "Gib Town."

"Pilgarlic" is written after a poem by poet Yehuda Amichai.

The following poems are dedicated to particular individuals: "Our Usual Place in the Universe" for Jay White; "A Blood Race" for Dave Spohn; "What the Hats Whisper" for Valerie Arrowsmith; "Laughing Falls" for Ryozo Morishita; "Roses and Thorns, Pots and Pans" for my daughter, Rose; and "Two Bodies" for Kay.

RICHARD SOLLY received summa cum laude masters degrees from Iowa State University and Hazelden Graduate School of Addiction Studies. His poetry and essays have won numerous awards, including four fellowships from the Minnesota State Arts Board, the Bush Foundation Artist Fellowship, the Loft–McKnight Award, and the Pearl Hogrefe Fellowship from Iowa State University. Other grants come from the Jerome Foundation, Louisiana Southern Poetry Prize, The Loft, Banff Centre for the Arts, Lake Superior Regional Writers Series, FORECAST Public Artworks, and the Third Century Poetry and Prose Award from the University of Minnesota. He has authored/coauthored three books. His poems have appeared in a variety of magazines. He currently works as a senior acquisitions editor for Hazelden Publishing, teaches creative writing at The Loft Literary Center, and does community service work in the areas of hospice and arts-in-health care. He lives in St. Paul, Minnesota, with his daughter.